The Reluctant Cook

The Reluctant Cook

Helen B. Gustafson

CELESTIAL ARTS • BERKELEY, CALIFORNIA

Acknowledgments

To the suggesters, tasters, and readers who were so generous with their time—a big helping of thanks: Elizabeth Ashe, Joyce Brekke, Lynne Cahoon, Lona Coleman, Barbara Costa, Marion Cunningham, Narsai David, Adrienne Demarest, Carol Field, Jovita Fitzgerald, Margaret Fox, M. F. K. Fisher, Barbara Foukes, Mimi Franks, Audrey Greenwood, Glenna Gregg, Mimi Groushong, Bertha Gustafson, Shelley Handler, Mijó Horwich, John Hudspeth, Robert Kratz, Irene McGill, Mag Moulton, Myrtle Nieder, Ellen Siegelman, Judith Stronach, Frank Roseberry, Emily Warden, Michael Wild, Barbara Wolfinger, Sandra Wooten, and my thanks to Eleanor Daigler for special research.

CELESTIAL ARTS
P.O. Box 7327
Berkeley, California 94707

First Printing, 1990
Library of Congress Catalog Card Number: 90-81085
ISBN 0-89087-594-4
Manufactured in the United States of America

Design by Patricia Curtan
Cover design by Patricia Curtan
Cover photography by M. Lee Fatherree

She lived with us from the time I was six years old. Her breakfast was at 6:00 A.M., she served us at 7:00; morning snack was at 10:00, lunch at noon sharp. After lunch it was rest time from 1:30 to 2:30, then a change of clothes and she was a *lady*, reading Thomas Mann and Sandburg. Tea was at 4:00 in the sun room, the large tea tray on the piano bench. Often it was a dot of jam on an arrowroot biscuit if cookies had run out, but it was Tea. At 5:30 precisely she'd announce, "Now I'll get supper," and at 6:00 we sat down. No exceptions. I was amazed as a child to learn that other people ate at different times, and sometimes at different times within a week! The notion that supper could be at 7:00 was as likely as the house rising off its foundation. This routine was a comfort to me in lonely college days—just by looking at the clock I knew exactly what was going on at home.

This book is also for Uncle Walt, seminary student turned doctor, barrel-chested, brown-eyed—who knew how to accept the changes in life and, as he put it in his firm basso, "Make the adjustment." He would lustily boom a paraphrased version of Longfellow's *A Psalm of Life*:

Life is real! Life is earnest! Life is not an empty dream!

This little book addresses the "real and earnest" part. Cooking for yourself, *by* yourself, perhaps for the very first time, and making a success of it, is *quite* an adjustment—and no mean accomplishment.

I hope from the bottom of my heart, with a few tips from Muttie and Uncle Walt's resounding and very true words, to make the adjustment just a little bit easier.

H.B.G.

Dedication

To my maternal grandmother who, like all Austrian grandmothers, was known to us as "Muttie," and to Uncle Walt. Muttie and Walt were products of Methodist parsonage life at the turn of the century. It was a time of:

> Use it up, wear it out,
> Make it do, or do without.

Ministers in those days depended on the contributions of parishioners—an old pillow, a stack of dishtowels, a barrel of flour—to "make it do." Muttie had an intuitive sense of how to make something comforting and satisfying from the slimmest of ingredients. Uncle Walt recalls sitting on the back stairs just off the kitchen in the old shingled parsonage, at a time when sugar was in short supply, watching Muttie produce molasses cookies at an astonishing rate. Somehow, I absorbed some of this get-on-with-it frugality and it's been an angel on my shoulder ever since.

Muttie ran a tight ship. Many visiting firemen, the euphemism for any kind of visitor, came through the parsonage, and she'd have supper ready for three, five, or ten on very short notice. It was one pan for a main meal, one bowl for a cake, and icing that could be made in one minute—egg whites and powdered sugar, topped with coconut. It only lasted ten minutes, but the cake only lasted that long anyway.

She ran a household without a stop from the time she was ten years old; caring for her invalid mother and three brothers and sisters, she became a mountain of efficiency and dispatch. Bent with work, tiny and wiry, she never lost her sense of purpose or her smile. She always said, "Have a *profitable* time," not "Have a good time."

❖ Contents

❖ *Soups and Light Meals*

Leek and Potato Soup
Tomato Soup
Pick-me-up Soup
Chicken Broth
Risotto
Versatile Vegetable Dish
On-the-spot Pasta
Macaroni and Cheese
Muttie's Egg Sandwich
Frittata
Angie's Sweet Egg Lunch
Muttie's Salad
Parsley Salad with Bread Crumbs
Old Faithful Baked Potato Dinner
Roast New Potatoes and Garlic
Custardy French Toast for One
Milk Toast
Delicious High-protein Pancakes

Leek and Potato Soup

Only three ingredients are needed to make this popular soup, and everything goes into the pot at the same time. It freezes perfectly so you might want to double or triple the recipe and freeze it in one-serving amounts.

3 servings
start to finish: 45 minutes

3 leeks
3 red potatoes
6 cups chicken broth
Salt and pepper

❖ Trim the leeks: cut off the roots and top half of the green stalks. Split lengthwise and rinse thoroughly. Cut or snip them into small pieces, or any size that suits you. Wash the potatoes and cut into quarters.

❖ Put the chicken broth in a saucepan and add the leeks and potatoes. Bring to a simmer and taste the broth for salt, and season to your taste.

❖ Simmer gently; in 30 minutes the vegetables will be tender. Cook longer for a thicker soup. It can also be puréed for a perfectly smooth soup.

Tomato Soup

My cousin, Mary Ruth Biles, gave me the inspiration for this soup. She adds crispy bacon pieces to hers and makes it a meal. I add fresh herbs, celery, green pepper, or anything that's handy and fresh.

serves 2
start to finish: 15 minutes

1 slice whole wheat bread
15½-ounce can of stewed tomatoes
½ pint (1 cup) whipping cream*
1 tablespoon chopped fresh herbs: parsley, basil, marjoram, etc.
OPTIONAL: 1 slice bacon, cut in pieces and cooked
Slices of celery, green pepper, or other fresh vegetables

❖ Toast a slice of whole wheat bread and set aside.

❖ Pour a can of stewed tomatoes into a medium saucepan and place over low-medium heat.

❖ Add the cream, fresh herbs, and bacon or vegetable, if you like, and simmer for 10 minutes.

❖ Cut the toast into bite-sized pieces. Ladle the soup into warmed bowls and place the croutons on top.

*Milk or half-and-half can be used—the texture suffers, but the taste is still delicious.

Pick-me-up Soup

There is a traditional Italian country soup very simply made with good chicken broth, eggs, Parmesan cheese, and bread-crumbs. This is a variation of that soup made with lemon and spinach. Its clean taste is invigorating and it can be made at the drop of a hat.

serves 1
start to finish: 15 minutes

2 cups homemade chicken broth; or, canned chicken broth
Salt and pepper
1 lemon
1 egg
½ bunch fresh spinach leaves, de-stemmed and washed; or,
½ box frozen spinach, thawed

❖ Put the broth in a saucepan and heat to a simmer. Taste for salt and season if needed. Add the juice of 1 lemon to taste. The soup should be quite tart at this point.

❖ Crack the egg into a small bowl, season with pepper, and add a tablespoon or so of cooled broth. Beat thoroughly with a fork.

❖ When the broth is boiling gently, slowly pour in the egg, gently whisking the broth all the while with the fork. The egg will set quickly in threadlike strands.

❖ Lower the heat to a very gentle simmer and add the spinach. Cook for 3 or 4 minutes until the greens are tender and wilted, and it's ready.

Chicken Broth

Homemade broth is well worth the extra effort and attention it takes to make it. If you have a large pot and can make a quantity of it at one time, that is the best way. Then you can freeze containers of broth to have on hand for soups, risotto, and stews.

I save carcasses of chicken and necks, wings, extra parts, either raw or roasted, in the freezer until I have enough to make broth. Try to have a mixture of meaty and skeletal parts, trimmed of fat, and if some are roasted, so much the better for flavor.

makes 3 quarts
start to finish: 3 to 4 hours

3 pounds chicken parts: carcasses, necks, backs, legs, etc.
3½ quarts cold water
1 teaspoon salt
1 carrot
1 stalk celery
1 onion
A few sprigs parsley
1 bay leaf
1 sprig thyme
A few black peppercorns

❖ Put the chicken parts in a large pot, add the water, and season with salt.

❖ Heat to boiling then immediately lower the heat to a gentle simmer. As it simmers for the first 15 minutes or so, skim off the fat and froth that comes to the surface. Then add the remaining vegetables and herbs and let simmer for about 3 hours.

❖ Turn off the heat and let it cool a while so that it is easier to handle. I find the easiest way to strain the broth is to lift out the chicken and vegetables with a big flat strainer or slotted spoon into a bowl, leaving the broth in the pot. Then pour or ladle the broth through a strainer into the containers that will store the broth in the refrigerator or freezer.

Put the chicken and vegetable remains in a double plastic bag to avoid leaks in the garbage.

The broth will keep well for 3 or 4 days in the refrigerator and up to 6 months in the freezer.

Risotto

Risotto always hits the spot. It is the method of cooking the rice that makes it so delicious. First the rice is cooked in butter and olive oil to give it a toasted flavor. Then two separate additions of simmering broth concentrate the flavor and give the rice a silky texture.

Endless variations are possible with this dish. Add chopped leftover chicken or meat in the last few minutes of cooking, or sliced raw vegetables midway in the cooking; you can be as creative as you wish, or as plain. Try it with a glass of red wine. Go on!

1 large or 2 medium servings start to finish: 30 minutes

2 cups chicken broth
OPTIONAL: salt
½ onion, diced or chopped
2 teaspoons butter
2 teaspoons olive oil
1 bay leaf
OPTIONAL: sprig fresh thyme
1 clove garlic
Black pepper
½ cup short-grain white rice, or Arborio rice
1 tablespoon Parmesan cheese
1 tablespoon parsley or basil, chopped

❖ Put the chicken broth in a pan and bring to a simmer. Taste the broth for salt. If needed, add salt to your liking.

❖ Dice or chop half an onion and put in a separate saucepan with butter, olive oil, bay leaf, thyme, and garlic. Cook over medium heat for 5 to 8 minutes, stirring occasionally. Season with pepper.

❖ Add the rice to the pan and continue cooking, stirring frequently for 4 to 5 minutes.

❖ Then add 1 cup of the simmering broth to the rice; you will hear the hissing and bubbling that is characteristic of this dish. Reduce the heat so that the rice is gently bubbling, and cook, uncovered, stirring occasionally, until almost all the liquid is absorbed, about 10 minutes.

❖ Add the remaining hot broth, increase the heat a bit, and continue to cook for approximately 10 minutes more. Taste the rice and when it is just tender it is done. Correct the seasoning with salt and pepper if needed. There will be a soupy texture to the rice and broth—that's what makes it so good!

❖ Serve in warm soup plates and sprinkle Parmesan cheese and chopped parsley or basil over the top.

Versatile Vegetable Dish

This vegetable dish is the equivalent of the simply cut, black "little nothing" dress of the fashion world—terribly useful, flexible, fresh, understated, and elegant.

It's a layered concoction of vegetables, some cooked longer to soften and some cooked briefly to retain their crispness. It can be transformed into a chunky vegetable soup by adding chicken broth, or puréed into a smooth soup.

serves 2 to 4
start to finish: 40 minutes

1 tablespoon olive oil
1 onion, sliced
2 or 3 garlic cloves, peeled and halved
10-ounce package of frozen lima beans or peas
1 teaspoon basil, fresh or dried
2 to 3 cups chopped tomatoes
1 zucchini, sliced, or 2 cups mushrooms, sliced
1 medium-sized head of Romaine lettuce, cut in bite-sized pieces

❖ First prepare and slice all the vegetables.

❖ Place a heavy stew pot, approximately 6 quart capacity, over low heat. Pour the olive oil into the pot, and add the onions, garlic, and limas or peas. Cover the pot and cook until the onions are just tender, about 10 minutes.

❖ Next, add the zucchini or mushrooms and season with salt and pepper. Turn the heat up a bit for these more substantial vegetables. Cook 5 minutes or so, stirring occasionally.

❖ Finally, add the tomatoes and lettuce, reduce the heat to low again, and cook for another 10 minutes. Give it all a stir and serve with grated Parmesan on top.

Note: For soup, add heated chicken broth; for a creamy soup, blend in batches in a food processor or blender until the desired consistency is obtained. This keeps in the refrigerator for 6 or 7 days and is good both hot and cold.

On-the-spot Pasta

A delicious recipe devised by the son of the great tenor Enrico Caruso is the inspiration for this quickest-of-all pasta. Place herbs, cheeses, and a bit of butter into a warmed soup plate, then add hot linguine, or, my favorite, wide egg noodles, and toss to coat the pasta. This can be done right at the table, and there you are with hardly a dish to wash!

serves 2
start to finish: 20 minutes

4 ounces dry linguine or wide egg noodles
1 tablespoon olive oil, or vegetable oil
½ cup Parmesan cheese, grated
¼ cup chopped chives, green onions, parsley, basil, or
    other herbs
4 tablespoons fresh ricotta cheese
2 tablespoons butter
Salt and pepper

❖ Turn the oven on to 250° and place two soup plates on the middle shelf to warm.

❖ Put approximately 2 quarts of water into a large pot, add a teaspoon of salt, 1 tablespoon oil, and bring to a rolling boil.

❖ Add the pasta. Cook, stirring occasionally, until tender but firm, about 8 to 12 minutes. While the pasta boils prepare the herbs and cheeses.

❖ Grate the Parmesan cheese into a bowl. Make a generous amount, slightly over ½ cup for two people so there will be extra to serve at the table. Wash and chop the chives or other herbs.

❖ Use a towel to remove the soup plates from the oven and put into each a tablespoon or two of ricotta cheese, a sprinkling of herbs, a tablespoon of butter, and a heaping tablespoon of Parmesan. (At this point, I often add fresh tomato slices to the side of the bowl—pretty and good.)

❖ Check the pasta now by tasting one strand. If tender, but still a little firm, drain the pasta in a colander in the sink. Serve the pasta directly into the soup plates and season with salt and pepper. Stir and toss *right at the table* and keep the Parmesan close by to add a finishing touch.

Note: As a festive alternative, or an "ice-breaker" for a few friends, place the bowls with the butter, Parmesan, and chives *right on the table*, and friends and family can make their own pasta dish right on the spot. If you do so, be sure to double or triple the ingredients!

Macaroni and Cheese

After making this for my kids, sometimes two or three times a day, this method evolved, with the help of Alma Hagge, our Swedish babysitter. I used to fret with frustration while she laughed her big laugh and made it easier and easier. It is the fastest, simplest, and most foolproof way.

serves 1 generously
start to finish: 20 minutes

¼ teaspoon salt
4 ounces elbow macaroni; or
3 ounces egg noodles
2 to 3 ounces cheddar cheese

❖ Fill a medium saucepan three-quarters full with cold water. Add ¼ teaspoon salt to the water. Put it on a burner over high heat. When it boils add the macaroni or noodles. Turn the heat down to medium and boil for 8 to 12 minutes. Do not cover.

❖ Grate ¾ cup cheese into a small plate.

❖ After 8 minutes or so of cooking, test the macaroni for doneness. Lift some out with a slotted spoon, let cool for a moment, and taste. If they are soft and tender, they're done. If not soft, cook 2 or 3 minutes longer.

❖ Put a colander in the sink and pour the macaroni into it. Plop the drained macaroni back into the hot saucepan, add the cheese, give it a stir, and put the lid back on it.

❖ Make yourself wait 5 minutes before you eat, to allow the cheese to melt. Then it's ready!

Muttie's Egg Sandwich

When my Austrian grandmother (grösmutter, thus the name Muttie) was out of steam, ideas, or groceries, she would announce that she would just have "n'egg" for lunch—it sounded like one word to my ears.

A lightly toasted, buttery scrambled egg sandwich is what it is, and very good, too.

serves 1
start to finish: 15 minutes

2 slices good quality white bread
1 tablespoon butter or oil
2 eggs
salt and pepper

❖ Toast the bread so that it is just crisp, not even *lightly* browned. Butter the toast and keep it warm.

❖ Heat a small frying pan, add a teaspoon of butter or oil, and break in 2 eggs. Stir them around vigorously, breaking the yolks to make a quick scramble. Cook until just done—moist eggs taste best, I think.

❖ When done, plop the eggs onto a slice of toast, season with salt and pepper to taste, and top with the other slice of toast. Press down so the toast absorbs the butter and eggs. Cut in half and there you have it.

Note: If you like something zippy try adding some Ortega roasted chilies or strips of good anchovies to your sandwich.

Frittata

Frittata is a hearty vegetable omelet baked in the oven, and can be eaten hot, cold, or in between. When a wave of energy appears, put this together and you'll have something tasty on hand and ready to eat. It will keep well in the refrigerator for 5 to 6 days.

4 servings
start to finish: 1 hour and 20 minutes

3 small red potatoes
3 or 4 small zucchini
1 or 2 slices fresh bread, for bread crumbs
3 cloves garlic
5 to 6 sprigs parsley
5 eggs
¼ cup good quality Parmesan cheese, grated
2 tablespoons melted butter
½ teaspoon fresh oregano
4 slices cheddar cheese
4 slices tomato

❖ Preheat the oven to 375°.

❖ Prepare the vegetables, bread, and herbs: Wash the potatoes, leave the skins on, and cut in quarters. Boil until almost tender, then drain.

❖ Slice the zucchini to yield approximately 2 cups.

❖ Cut the bread into smaller pieces and process in a blender or food processor to make ½ cup fresh bread crumbs.

❖ Peel the garlic and slice thinly. Chop the parsley.

❖ In a large mixing bowl, beat the eggs, then add the potatoes, zucchini, bread crumbs, garlic, parsley, Parmesan cheese, and melted butter.

❖ Stir everything together and pour into a buttered or oiled 8-inch Pyrex or earthenware dish. Sprinkle the oregano on top.

❖ Bake for 45 minutes. Then cover the top with slices of cheddar cheese, top with tomato slices, turn the thermostat up to 475°, and bake for another 10 minutes.

❖ Cut into squares and serve alone, with a green salad, or as an accompaniment to almost any meat dish.

Angie's Sweet Egg Lunch

Sometimes when I know I need to eat but don't have much appetite, I make this for lunch. It never fails to please and always perks me up. A very sophisticated Angie gave me this recipe—she got it from her grandmother.

serves 1
start to finish: 20 to 30 minutes

½ cup fresh or frozen peas
1 egg
Butter
Salt

❖ Preheat the oven to 350°.

❖ Pour about ½ cup peas into a small oven-proof dish or ramekin, four inches or so in diameter. Break an egg on top of the peas.

❖ Place the ramekin in the oven for approximately 20 minutes, or until the white looks and feels fairly firm. If you like a soft egg, check it at 15 minutes. If you like a hard egg, check it at 25 minutes.

❖ Remove the ramekin from the oven to a plate. Dot the egg with butter, season with salt, and enjoy.

The spoonbread recipe on page 59 makes a good accompaniment.

Muttie's Salad

Muttie, my grandmother, always said she fairly stood over the leaf lettuce in the spring, so eager was she for fresh greens. At age ten she routinely made this salad for her whole family. In my youth, it was usually served on Sunday and always in a glass bowl.

serves 2 to 4
start to finish: 15 minutes

2 small heads leaf or butter lettuce
1 small bunch green onions
½ to ¾ cup half-and-half or whipping cream
2 tablespoons cider vinegar
1 tablespoon sugar

❖ Wash, drain, and tear the lettuce and place in a bowl.

❖ Trim the green onions and cut into ¼-inch pieces, including some of the green stalk. Add to the lettuce.

❖ Pour in ½ to ¾ cup half-and-half or cream. Add the vinegar and sprinkle on the sugar.

❖ Toss well and taste. (Muttie always put her finger in.) If too sweet add vinegar, if too sharp add sugar to your liking, give it another stir, and serve.

If the salad stands a while it gets soggy, but that's alright, it's even more delicious as a wilted lettuce salad.

Parsley Salad with Bread Crumbs

Parsley is high in vitamins and very nutritious.

serves 1
start to finish: 30 minutes

1 slice crusty country-style bread or French bread
1 bunch parsley
1 clove garlic
1 tablespoon red wine vinegar
3 tablespoons good olive oil
Salt and pepper

❖ Preheat the oven or toaster oven to 350°. Cut the bread into small pieces and process in a blender or food processor to make bread crumbs. Spread the crumbs out on a baking tray and dry in the oven for 15 minutes or so until lightly browned and crisp. During the cooking, use a spatula to turn over and stir the crumbs a few times. Set aside.

❖ De-stem and wash the parsley, then dry it well. Chill in the refrigerator.

❖ Make the dressing: Smash the clove of garlic a bit, slip off the skin, and put the garlic in a small bowl to marinate in the vinegar. After 10 minutes remove the garlic and whisk in the olive oil. Taste and add more vinegar or oil as necessary.

❖ Now combine the parsley and dressing, a bit of salt and pepper, and toss well. Add the bread crumbs and toss well again and serve.

This salad is also good with grated cheese instead of bread crumbs. Add some sliced tomatoes, hard-cooked egg, fresh salad vegetables, and you have a fine summer meal.

Old Faithful Baked Potato Dinner

Sometimes just one simple thing is all that's wanted for dinner. A baked potato, eaten with the skin on and a little cheese, is a nutritionally balanced, complete meal—probably the world's first comfort food.

serves 1
start to finish: 1 hour and 30 minutes

1 baking potato
2 tablespoons, or to taste, butter or oil
1 to 2 ounces cheddar cheese, grated or sliced
Salt and pepper

❖ One hour and fifteen minutes before you want to eat, turn the oven on to 400°. Wash and prick the potato and put it in the oven.

❖ After 1 hour and 15 minutes, remove the potato from the oven, slice it open, and add the butter or oil, and cheese. Season with salt and pepper to taste.

❖ Wrap the potato in foil and return to the oven for 10 minutes to let the cheese melt into the potato, then eat!

Roast New Potatoes and Garlic

Small potatoes and fresh garlic, both baked in their jackets, are a perfect combination. If you've never tasted garlic cooked this way, you don't know what you are missing. When garlic is cooked gently and long the flavor becomes very sweet and refined. Even people who say they don't like garlic love it this way.

I like to cook this in the spring and summer when the potatoes and garlic are at their best.

serves 2
start to finish: 1 hour

10 or 12 new potatoes
Bay leaf, fresh thyme, or rosemary
1 head garlic
2 tablespoons olive oil
Salt and pepper
OPTIONAL: butter or fresh pot cheese

❖ Preheat the oven to 325°.

❖ Wash the potatoes and put them in an earthenware or oven-proof dish. Add a few bay leaves and a few sprigs of fresh herbs.

❖ Separate the head of garlic into individual cloves, but do not peel. Add the cloves to the dish. Drizzle the potatoes and garlic with olive oil, season with salt and pepper, and stir a bit.

❖ Bake for about 1 hour; stir occasionally. When the potatoes and garlic are both tender, they're done.

The nice way to eat this is to squeeze the garlic, which is soft like butter, out of the skin and spread it on the steamy potatoes. You can enrich the meal with an addition of butter or fresh mild cheese.

Custardy French Toast for One

My favorite beauty operator in the world, Barbara Costa, handed over this delightful supper dish after being reassured that "something too simple to write down" was exactly what I wanted.

The extra egg and half-and-half added at the end gives not only added protein, but a luxurious custardy finish. After a long day this is just right.

serves 1
start to finish: 20 minutes

2 eggs
2 tablespoons milk
½ teaspoon vanilla
2 slices French bread, or white bread
½ teaspoon butter or oil
2 tablespoons half-and-half or cream
Syrup, jam, or fruit preserves

❖ In a shallow soup plate or pie tin, beat together 1 egg, the milk, and vanilla. Put 2 slices of bread in this mixture and let them soak for a few minutes on each side.

❖ Place an 8-inch or 9-inch frying pan that has a lid over medium heat. Next put about ½ teaspoon of butter or oil in the pan and swirl it around. Place the bread slices side by side in the pan and let them cook gently for 3 or 4 minutes, a bit longer if the bread slices are very thick.

❖ While the bread is cooking, mix the other egg with about 2 tablespoons of half-and-half or cream in a small bowl. Pour this mixture over the top of both slices of bread and put the lid on the pan.

❖ Turn down the heat to low and let it all cook together for another minute or two.

❖ Take a peek! If the custardy part surrounding the bread looks set, it's done. If it is still a bit liquid, replace the lid and cook another minute. Remove from the heat and lift out with a spatula.

❖ Serve on a warmed plate with syrup, jam, preserves, or cinnamon and sugar. If your appetite is good and you have a slice of ham in the refrigerator, slip it into the still warm pan for a minute and eat it along with the French toast.

Milk Toast

Each version of milk toast inspires fierce loyalty. It is said that George Bernard Shaw became indignant when a recipe dissimilar to his own—not even intended for him—was made in his presence.

This variation has been a mainstay in our family forever, and I believe it is, of course, the only true and perfect one.

serves 1
start to finish: 10 minutes

1 slice good quality bread
1 cup milk
1 teaspoon sugar
¼ to ½ teaspoon cinnamon to taste, or,
OPTIONAL: salt and pepper to taste

❖ Toast the bread lightly.

❖ Put in a large, warmed soup plate and cut into bite-sized pieces.

❖ Now heat the milk *almost* to boiling and pour down the *side* of the dish so the tops of the toast pieces remain crisp.

❖ Sprinkle with the sugar and cinnamon, or salt and pepper if you prefer, make some tea, and enjoy a classic.

Delicious High-protein Pancakes

I spied this recipe in a famous cookbook put out by the Junior League of Baton Rouge, Louisiana. Mrs. Ross Munson contributed the recipe. The River Road Recipes II has sold 350,000 copies a year since 1976, a true fundraiser.

The ingredients are staples in many households; and these pancakes really are delicious.

serves 1 or 2
start to finish: 15 minutes

2 eggs
½ cup cottage cheese
1 tablespoon oil
¼ cup uncooked oatmeal; or,
⅛ cup oatmeal and ⅛ cup wheat germ
⅛ teaspoon salt

❖ Place all ingredients in a blender or food processor and blend for 5 to 6 seconds.

❖ Drop by tablespoons onto a hot, greased frying pan. Turn the pancakes when bubbles appear on the surface, and cook 1 minute more.

❖ Serve with jam, fruit preserves, fresh berries, or other fruit. Surprisingly, these pancakes taste much better with fruit than with syrup.

❖ Quick Fish, Hot and Cold

Salmon Spectacular with Green Onions
The Easiest Poached Salmon
Broiled Halibut with Tangy Yogurt Sauce
Home-style Fish Chowder
Foil Fish
Sole Madison
Tuna Antipasto Plate
Hot Weather Salad

Salmon Spectacular with Green Onions

Crusty, crisp, delicious, and quite a different taste than other salmon dishes. Serve with some new potatoes boiled in their skins, plain rice, or steamed vegetables and have a feast for one.

Shelley Handler, Bay Area cooking teacher, mentioned this down-home secret in passing . . . so I pass it along.

serves 1
start to finish: 30 minutes

2 or 3 small new potatoes
2 or 3 tablespoons good olive oil
4 green onions
1 salmon steak or fillet
Salt and pepper
Lemon wedge
Butter
1 teaspoon chopped parsley

❖ Wash the potatoes and put them on to boil. When they start to soften, in about 10 minutes, begin to cook the salmon.

❖ Pour 2 to 3 tablespoons olive oil into a large heavy frying pan over medium heat. Wash, then trim the ends from the green onions, leaving them whole, and place in the pan.

❖ Serve the salmon and onion with a wedge of lemon. Butter the potatoes on the plate, sprinkle with parsley, and season with salt and pepper to taste.

Don't worry if the onions brown—they're supposed to and they'll taste marvelous.

❖ Season the salmon with salt and pepper and add to the pan. Fry until crusty and thoroughly cooked, about 10 minutes depending on the thickness. There's no need to turn it over. Check the fish by inserting a small knife in the center; if the flesh has changed from dark pink to pale pink, it's done.

The Easiest Poached Salmon

The easiest way I know to cook tender and delicate salmon, and especially good if you have fresh dill.

serves 1
start to finish: 35 minutes

1 salmon fillet or steak
½ to ¾ cup half-and-half or milk
½ teaspoon chives, basil, or chopped fresh dill
Salt

❖ Preheat the oven to 350°.

❖ Place the salmon in a shallow oven dish and pour in the half-and-half or milk so that the fish is half immersed.

❖ Sprinkle with chives, basil, or dill and season with salt if you like.

❖ Bake for 30 minutes, occasionally spooning some of the half-and-half or milk over the salmon. To check for doneness, cut into the center a bit. When the fish is mostly pale pink but still a little bit darker pink in the center, it is done.

Broiled Halibut with Tangy Yogurt Sauce

No sticky frying pan to wash; the fish can be broiled on foil, and the foil tossed away. The yogurt sauce makes a soft, bubbly topping that is not overly rich. It is also an excellent sauce for steamed broccoli or salad—good choices to accompany the fish.

serves 2
start to finish: 30 minutes

2 cups plain yogurt
½ teaspoon minced garlic
3 to 4 tablespoons lemon juice
2 fillets halibut, or similar firm white fish, ¾- to 1-inch thick

❖ Turn the oven on to broil. Then prepare the yogurt topping: in a bowl or pitcher, blend the yogurt, garlic, and lemon juice. This will make enough topping for the fish and vegetables or salad. If you don't use all of it, save it for another meal. It will keep for a week or so.

❖ Line the broiler pan with foil and place the fish on it. Spread half the yogurt sauce on the fish fillets.

❖ Put the fish under the broiler and cook for 10 minutes, then check for doneness. The yogurt topping will be a light golden color. Take a fork and separate a clean sliver of fish. If it "flakes," that is, is evenly white and pulls away evenly, it's done.

❖ Transfer to warm plates and serve with steamed broccoli or salad, and extra yogurt sauce to add at the table.

Home-style Fish Chowder

A clean and light-tasting fish stew, its secret ingredient is a healthy splash of wine vinegar added just at the end. It gives the mild soup a transforming zing.

serves 2
start to finish: 30 to 40 minutes

1 small red or yellow onion
1 to 2 tablespoons olive oil
1 large red potato
Salt and pepper
A few sprigs of fresh parsley, and fresh thyme or
    marjoram
3 cups water
½- to ¾-pound fresh fish fillet: halibut, sea bass,
    salmon, snapper, etc., or a combination, cut in 1-inch
    chunks
Wine vinegar to taste

❖ Cut the onion in half, peel and trim the ends, then cut into thick slices. Cook in a heavy saucepan in olive oil over medium heat while you prepare the potato.

❖ Peel and cut the uncooked potato into rough cubes. Add to the pan along with the herbs. Season with salt and pepper, and cook for 10 minutes or so, uncovered.

❖ Add the water, bring to a simmer, and cook gently another 10 minutes or so until the potatoes begin to soften.

❖ Then add the fish and a bit more salt, and cook gently another 10 minutes or so until the fish is cooked.

❖ Spoon the chowder into warm bowls, season with ground black pepper, and about 1 teaspoon of wine vinegar, to taste, for each bowl.

Serve with warm bread or dry toast.

Foil Fish

Cooking fish in a closed packet steams it very gently and traps all the flavors and aromas inside. This is a simple, no-mess method that will work with nearly any kind of fish.

serves 1
start to finish: 25 minutes

Aluminum foil
1 serving of fish: halibut, flounder, sole, salmon, etc.
2 to 3 teaspoons lemon juice
2 to 3 tablespoons butter
Salt and pepper
A few sprigs parsley, basil, dill, or fennel
OPTIONAL: chopped garlic, tomato salsa, or oil and
vinegar dressing

❖ Turn the oven to 350°.

❖ Place the fish in the middle of a 12-inch square piece of foil. Season the fish with lemon juice, leaves of parsley or other herbs, butter, salt, and pepper. Add some garlic, if you like, or substitute salsa or oil and vinegar dressing for the lemon-herb butter.

❖ Gather the edges of the foil together, folding the edges over as you do so to make a tightly closed packet.

❖ Put the packet on a baking sheet and bake for approximately 15 minutes.
Steam or sauté a few vegetables while the fish is in the oven for a simple complete meal.

Sole Madison

Deborah Madison came for tea, stayed for supper, and made this delicious quick fish supper for all of us. The sauce is made right in the pan in the spaces between the frying fish. Then it is scooped up with a spatula right onto the fillet, and served immediately. I've made sole this way ever since.

serves 1
start to finish: 10 minutes

½ cup all-purpose flour
¼ teaspoon each salt and pepper
2 small or 1 large fillet of sole
1 to 2 tablespoons olive oil
2 tablespoons butter
2 teaspoons capers, drained and rinsed
Lemon

❖ Blend the flour, salt, and pepper. Dredge the sole in flour and shake off the excess.

❖ Heat the oil in a skillet and slip in the sole. Cook for 2 to 3 minutes, then turn the fish. In the space between the fillets add the butter and capers, and a good squeeze of lemon.

❖ When the butter is just melted use a spatula to scoop the caper butter onto the fish, and serve right away.

Tuna Antipasto Plate

Are you looking for a refreshing, different way to serve tuna? This tastes as good as it looks—a perfect hot summer supper or appetizer. The exact ingredients are not important. Any combination of fresh raw salad vegetables will work very well.

serves 2
start to finish: 15 minutes

1 small can best quality tuna
3 to 4 tablespoons olive oil
Black pepper
1 tablespoon capers, rinsed in water and drained
12 to 18 black olives
1 large ripe tomato, cut in wedges
Radishes
1 stalk celery, sliced
OPTIONAL: ½ sweet red onion, thinly sliced, green
          pepper or red pepper, sliced
Lemon
Crusty French bread or crackers

❖ Open the can of tuna, drain, and invert it onto the center of a large pretty plate. Drizzle 1 to 2 tablespoons olive oil over the tuna and season with black pepper. Spoon over some capers, rinsed of their brine and drained. Then scatter olives all around.

❖ Arrange the vegetables around on the plate: ripe tomato wedges, crispy radishes, sliced celery, thinly sliced onion, sliced peppers—whatever you like.

❖ Then drizzle more olive oil over the vegetables, season with salt and pepper, squeeze some lemon juice over the tuna and all, and stand back and admire your work.

❖ Serve with a good crusty bread or crackers, and dig in.

Hot Weather Salad

When the weather suddenly turns too hot even to think of heating up the kitchen, try this. Crisp and cool, and just filling enough to satisfy. Make sure you always have canned salmon on hand!

serves 2
start to finish: 30 minutes

7- to 8-ounce can salmon
2 large lettuce leaves, or the equivalent in smaller leaves
1 large cucumber
½ cup plain yogurt
A few lemon wedges, fresh cracked pepper, dill,
    parsley, chives—any of these are welcome additions
A few breadsticks, crackers, or fresh bread

❖ Open a can of salmon and drain off the liquid.

❖ Take the skin off the salmon and break the meat into chunks about as big as a walnut. Set aside.

❖ Wash and dry the lettuce leaves and put one, or several smaller leaves on each dinner plate.

❖ Divide the salmon into 2 servings and place on the lettuce leaves. Put the plates in the refrigerator to chill.

❖ Peel the cucumber with a vegetable peeler and cut into small chunks.

❖ Pour the yogurt into a small bowl. Add the cucumber chunks, a few capers, chopped dill, or other flavorings and a dash of salt and pepper.

❖ Spoon about a quarter of the dressing over the salmon on each plate and refrigerate them all while you make a little iced tea or open a bottle of white wine to complement your salad.

❖ Serve with crisp breadsticks or crackers, or some fresh bread.

Note: For a slightly more substantial touch, add a few cubed boiled potatoes to the plate as well—a neat way to use leftover potatoes.

❖ *Hearty Suppers and Old Favorites*

Plain Baked Chicken
Narsai David's Chicken Stew
Three-hour Chicken Stew
Chicken with Roasted Red Peppers
Spoonbread
Old-fashioned Chicken Dinner
Couscous with Chicken and Dried Fruit
Turkey Pie
Sautéed Liver Strips with Onions
Tofu Steaks
Baked Winter Squash and Sausage Supper
Double Good Cabbage and Sausage
Marinated Flank Steak
Polenta
New Tuna Casserole
No Stress Rice

Plain Baked Chicken

I like roast chicken to be browned and crispy on the outside, and tender and moist on the inside. This method does it.

"It's always nice," my mother used to say, "to have a roast to cut from." This is excellent as a main dish and the extras provide tender meat to add to other meals.

serves 3 or 4
start to finish: 1 hour and 15 minutes

3½- to 4-pound chicken
Salt

❖ Preheat the oven to 350°.

❖ Wash the chicken inside and out, trim the excess fat from the openings, and salt the bird inside and out.

❖ There are 3 steps to cooking the chicken. First, place the chicken *breast-side down* on a cookie sheet or roasting pan, and bake for 20 minutes.

❖ After 20 minutes of cooking, turn the chicken over, *breast-side up*, and cook another 25 minutes.

❖ For the final 20 minutes' roasting, turn the oven up to 400°. Leave the chicken breast-side up.

❖ At the end of 65 minutes' roasting time the chicken will be crisp to a golden brown.

Note: This chicken is good hot or cold. Cook it ahead and refrigerate for up to 3 days. Slice the meat off the bone and add it to a salad, sandwich, or combine it with broth, rice, and vegetables for a hearty soup.

I like to warm the chicken meat in some broth or cream with some fresh herbs and pour it over steaming egg noodles for a light pasta supper. Grate a little cheese on top—it's super.

Narsai David's Chicken Stew

This simple mini-stew is one of the best short-order meals I know. It is easy to make for one person or several; no need to be exact about ingredients. It's a life-saver when you long for warm, comforting stew and are convinced you have no time to make it.

serves 1
start to finish: 45 minutes

2 small chicken pieces (wings, backs, or thighs)
¼ teaspoon salt
½ carrot
½ stalk celery
½ onion; or, 2 or 3 green onions
½ potato
1 or 2 sprigs parsley
1 clove garlic
2 whole peppercorns
1 bay leaf
2 cloves
1½ cups chicken broth
English muffin, whole-wheat toast, or other bread

❖ Trim the chicken of any excess skin, or cut it off altogether. Place the chicken in a medium sized pot and season with a little salt.

❖ Cut the carrot, celery, onion, and potato into small pieces and add to the pot. Pinch the leaves off a sprig or two of parsley and put them in, too.

❖ Peel the garlic, cut in half, and add to the pot along with the peppercorns and the bay leaf stuck with cloves.

❖ Last, pour in the chicken broth to just barely cover the chicken pieces. Heat and bring to a boil for a moment, then reduce the heat to a gentle simmer, and cover with a close-fitting lid.

❖ The stew will be ready in 30 minutes. Fish out the bay leaf and cloves. Taste for salt and season to taste. Serve in a large soup plate with toasted English muffin or whole-wheat bread.

Three-hour Chicken Stew

Don't be fooled by the ordinary title. This stew is plate-mopping good. It can be assembled all at once—no browning of the meat—and requires absolutely no fussing. It is an excellent dish to freeze in one-serving amounts.

serves 4
start to finish: 3 hours and 30 minutes

3- to 4-pound chicken, cut up; or 4 large pieces
3 or 4 white or red potatoes
3 or 4 carrots
1 onion
2 cloves garlic
OPTIONAL: a few sprigs fresh thyme and parsley
              1 green pepper
Salt and pepper
2 cups chicken broth
1 cup white or red wine
¼ to ⅓ cup tapioca or couscous

❖ Preheat the oven to 300°.

❖ Remove any excess skin from the chicken pieces. To avoid a fatty stew, at least half the pieces should be without skin.

❖ Put the chicken into a large deep-sided pot.

❖ Prepare the vegetables: wash and quarter the potatoes. Peel and cut the carrots into bite-size pieces. Peel and quarter the onion. Peel 2 cloves garlic. Fresh thyme and parsley, and a seeded and chopped green pepper are tasty additions.

❖ Add all the vegetables and herbs to the pot and season to taste with salt and pepper.

❖ Pour in the chicken broth and wine. Stir in the tapioca or couscous. Put the lid on the pot and braise in the oven for 3 hours.

❖ Serve with a good crusty bread, rice, or noodles.

Note: You can make an excellent beef stew by substituting 1 pound beef stewmeat (sirloin tip is very good) for the chicken. The procedure is just the same. I prefer red wine and beef broth, but chicken broth works just fine.

Chicken with Roasted Red Peppers

Staying in a cabin in the mountains, I looked at the dinner makings on the last day and saw a lone bottle of abandoned peppers (roasted sweet peppers, not hot chile peppers) and one cut-up chicken in the fridge.

With my favorite fast flourish of just putting two things together, I browned the chicken, poured the peppers and the liquid (everything but the lid is my motto) into the frying pan, clapped the lid on, and waited 45 minutes. Delicious.

4 servings
start to finish: 1 hour

1 tablespoon olive oil or vegetable oil
1 chicken cut into small pieces; or, 4 chicken breasts, with skins, quartered
7½-ounce jar roasted red peppers

❖ Preheat the oven to 375°.

❖ Heat a large, heavy oven-proof frying pan over medium-high heat, then add a tablespoon of oil.

❖ Lightly brown the chicken pieces on all sides.

❖ Pour the peppers, with the juices, over the chicken. Cover the pan with a lid, transfer to the oven, and bake for 45 minutes.

Note: Spoonbread is particularly good with this chicken and roasted pepper combination. It takes about half an hour to make, so if you start it when the chicken goes into the oven, they will be ready about the same time. Although spoonbread usually requires 400°, it bakes nicely at 375°.

Spoonbread

Spoonbread is soft cornbread, with the center almost like pudding. It can be a meal in itself or makes a great accompaniment to sausages, meat, roast chicken, eggs, vegetables, or almost anything.

serves 2
start to finish: 35 minutes

1 egg
1⅓ cups milk
8½-ounce package commercial cornbread mix (1⅓ cups)

❖ Preheat the oven to 400°.

❖ Beat the egg in an ungreased 8-inch casserole dish. Add the milk and the cornbread mix and stir until the batter is smooth. Do not beat. (For a more delicate texture, add an extra egg white to the batter.)

❖ Bake for 30 to 35 minutes. When done, the outside will be set like cornbread and the center will be soft and slightly sunken.

❖ When there is spoonbread for supper many people will pass up dessert and finish the spoonbread with syrup.

Note: Leftover bits of chicken, sausage, or anything that appeals may be added to the bowl before the batter.

Old-fashioned Chicken Dinner

Some folks get downright cranky unless they have mashed potatoes along with their Sunday chicken dinner, but mashed potatoes always seem so time consuming. This recipe offers a shortcut. A very liquid instant mashed potato mixture is poured over chicken pieces in a shallow pan. The chicken bakes and the potatoes rise high and fluffy, and lightly browned. I think it's terrific with nuts or raisins on the bottom, but for the traditionalist, keep it simple.

serves 4
start to finish: 35 minutes

1 small stalk celery
4 chicken breasts, de-boned
Salt and pepper
1 or 1⅓ cups instant mashed potatoes made with 2 cups
    milk, depending on the brand; or,
3 cups fresh mashed potatoes, made practically
    pourable with extra milk
3 to 4 tablespoons Parmesan cheese
OPTIONAL: ¼ cup walnuts, water chestnuts, or currants
        and raisins

❖ Preheat the oven to 500°.

❖ Cut the celery into ½-inch slices and scatter them on the bottom of a 10-inch cast-iron frying pan.

❖ Place the chicken breast in the pan, skin-side up. (Remove the skin for cholesterol-conscious folk.) Season chicken with salt and pepper, approximately ¼ teaspoon.

❖ Make instant mashed potatoes for four following the directions on the package, *but add 2 cups milk* instead of the ⅓ or ⅔ cup called for; or make 3 cups fresh mashed potatoes thinned with extra milk—it should be almost liquid.

❖ Pour the potato mixture over the chicken and sprinkle Parmesan cheese on top.

❖ Bake for 20 to 25 minutes until the potatoes are nicely browned.

❖ To serve, scoop out a serving of chicken with potatoes on top for each plate. Don't forget the good juices on the bottom of the pan.

Note: Walnuts or water chestnuts in place of the celery add a nice crunchiness. If you like a more delicate texture, try currants and raisins; they make a sweet sort of gravy on the bottom of the pan—it's my favorite.

This can also be made with turkey or chicken breasts on the bone. If so, add about 10 minutes to the baking time.

If I do this recipe, I can put chicken on ½ the pan & nuts, etc. on the other ½ (since Marc doesn't like nuts) & the cheese on top of "my ½" would be the clue as to which was which — a salad & simple hot vegie, with bread for me (& Marc, if he wanted) would make the meal.

Couscous with Chicken and Dried Fruit

I had been dreaming of some quickly made, gentle and satisfying meal for years. I finally found it in a brief conversation with Michael Wild, Bay Area restaurateur, standing with our shopping carts nose to nose in the grocery store. I'm convinced that the best recipes are exchanged this way.

Couscous may sound like an adventure to you, but after all, why not? It is durum wheat (semolina) milled to a granular texture. You may be more familiar with this grain as macaroni or, a breakfast favorite, Cream of Wheat. Couscous, when cooked, is a light, fluffy, delicate grain, like fine rice.

serves 2
start to finish: 20 minutes

3 tablespoons olive oil
¼ yellow onion
1 cup chicken broth
½ cup couscous, medium or fine grade
1 cooked chicken breast, cut in bite-size pieces;
   or,
½ to ¾ cup stewed lamb, beef, or sausages
¼ to ½ cup raisins
OPTIONAL: moist dried apricots and/or prunes,
         cut in pieces
         Yogurt

❖ Put the olive oil in a heavy-bottomed pot, or frying pan, that has a lid, and place over medium heat.

❖ Cut a quarter of an onion into slices and sauté gently in the oil for 4 to 5 minutes. Stir occasionally until they become transparent, but do not brown.

❖ Add the broth to the pot and bring to a simmer.

❖ Add the couscous, chicken, or meat, and raisins—or whatever combination you like—to the broth. Cover and cook gently for 5 minutes, until all the broth is absorbed and the couscous is fluffy and dry.

Serve as is or with plain yogurt on the side.

Note: For a lighter and quicker version you can eliminate the oil and onions, and make a simpler combination of ingredients, like chicken and apricots, or chickpeas and squash, etc.

For those who like an all-vegetable dish, this is an excellent base. Add a mixture of steamed vegetables: squash, onion, sweet potato, chickpeas, beans, etc.

Turkey Pie

A *take-off on the old shepherd's pie theme, this variation is mild and delicate.*

serves 2
start to finish: 25 minutes

¼ to ⅓ pound ground turkey
8½-ounce package cornbread mix, or 1⅓ cups
1 egg
¼ cup milk
OPTIONAL: applesauce or cranberry sauce

❖ Preheat the oven to 400°.

❖ Pat ground turkey into the bottom of a 7- or 8-inch casserole—no need to grease the pan or to use salt and pepper.

❖ Make a cornbread batter following the directions on the package, using the egg and milk (or spoonbread batter, page 59).

❖ Pour or spread the batter on top of the ground turkey, and bake, uncovered, for 20 minutes. Serve it hot from the oven with a little butter on top, or applesauce or cranberry sauce on the side.

Sautéed Liver Strips with Onion

Tender pink calf liver sautéed this way is entirely different than a floured and fried version. It's opened the eyes of many a hardened liver hater. I am grateful to Raymond Sokolov who inspired this recipe.

serves 1
After liver is milk-soaked for a couple of hours:
start to finish: 10 minutes

½ pound calf liver
1 cup milk
1 yellow or red onion
1 tablespoon butter or oil
1 tablespoon vegetable or olive oil
Salt and pepper

❖ Trim away the membrane from the edge of the liver. Soak the liver in milk for a couple of hours.

❖ Peel and slice the onion into thin rings.

❖ Heat a frying pan over medium heat, then add the butter or oil. Add the onion rings to the pan and cook, stirring occasionally, until they turn translucent—slightly brown is good, too, but stronger tasting.

❖ Drain the liver and cut into ¼-inch strips. Add to the pan with the onions and season with salt and pepper. Sauté until the liver is cooked but still a bit pink, about 3 to 4 minutes.

❖ Remove from the pan right away and serve with parsley salad and bread crumbs (see page 28), or polenta.

Tofu Steaks

Tofu is made from soy beans and is one of the best, least fatty, and most inexpensive sources of protein. Here the tofu is cooked in a tasty mixture of garlic, olive oil, and soy sauce. If you have a choice at the market between the "silky" smooth tofu, or the "regular" coarse variety, choose the regular kind. The little irregular holes allow the marinade to soak into the tofu—essential for good flavor.

Garnished with radishes this dish is quite festive—good enough for "second-best company," as Muttie used to say. Second-best company is in definite contrast to Big Company, such as the minister or relatives from any town larger than the one in which you reside.

serves 2
start to finish: 50 minutes

2 ½ cups water
½ teaspoon salt
½ teaspoon butter or oil
1 cup brown rice
8 ounces "regular" tofu
4 tablespoons olive oil
1 teaspoon minced garlic
3 tablespoons "light" soy sauce
OPTIONAL: a few radishes, small celery stalk, small bunch watercress, or water chestnuts

❖ In a medium saucepan combine the water, salt, and butter or oil. When the water comes to a full boil, slowly add the brown rice. Continue to boil for a few minutes, then cover and reduce the heat to a simmer. The rice will take about 40 minutes to cook. After about 20 minutes, start to prepare the rest of the meal.

❖ Drain the tofu. Cut into slices about ½-inch thick and place on a paper towel to dry.

❖ Heat the olive oil in a heavy skillet over medium heat. Add the garlic and soy sauce and stir. Now add the tofu slices and let them cook gently. Turn them over now and then as you prepare the vegetables. The tofu can cook from 10 to 20 minutes and will turn a nutty brown, like a steak.

❖ Wash and slice the radishes and/or celery. Wash and cut the watercress or other greens. Toasted walnuts are a delicious addition.

❖ When the rice is tender, spoon steaming mounds onto each plate, add the tofu, and pour any remaining juices over the top. Sprinkle with radishes, celery, greens, walnuts, or whatever combination of garnishes you choose.

Baked Winter Squash and Sausage Supper

Baked winter squash is particularly inviting in the fall and early winter months. The sugars in the squash ooze out during the baking and caramelize, which smells heavenly and tastes even better. It is an inexpensive supper and adds good fiber to the diet. Mag Moulton, from Minneapolis, Minnesota suggested this recipe.

serves 2
start to finish: 1 hour and 15 minutes

1 acorn or butternut squash—almost any size will do (do not substitute banana squash)
1 to 2 tablespoons brown sugar
2 pork sausages (link is the best shape—use 2 or 3 sausages for a hearty meal)
1 cup water

❖ One hour and 15 minutes before you want to eat, turn the oven on to 400°.

❖ Line a cookie sheet with sides, or a roasting pan, with aluminum foil. This makes for an easier cleanup later.

❖ Cut the squash in half lengthwise and scoop out the stringy pulp and seeds. Pat about 1 tablespoon brown sugar into the hollow center of each half. Tuck a sausage or sausages in the center of each.

❖ Place the squash halves cut-side down on the foil. Put in the oven and pour about 1 cup water into the pan.

❖ After 1 hour, the squash will be very tender and the juices nicely caramelized. Transfer the squash and sausage to plates with a large spatula, scoop the soft squash out of the skins like a melon, and enjoy.

Note: For those who prefer a meatless meal, this squash dish is very satisfying without the sausage. You can also make a fine soup if you scoop out the squash and mix it with warm chicken broth; just add broth until you have the desired consistency. The squash is already a soft purée and will blend easily with the broth.

Double Good Cabbage and Sausages

Cabbage and sausage is a time-honored tradition in Europe, and for good reason! The flavor of cabbage is enhanced by savory meat juices and together they make a healthy and wholesome meal. Here is an uncomplicated version that is very good and is easy to prepare.

This is also delicious without the sausages—use caraway seed instead of mustard seed.

serves 2
start to finish: 45 minutes

4 small or 2 large sausages of your choice
½ head of cabbage
1 tablespoon mustard seed
½ to ¼ cup water or white wine

❖ Cook the sausages in a large heavy pot over medium heat, for about 10 to 15 minutes, until nicely browned. Turn the sausages during the cooking. Drain off excess fat.

❖ While the sausage is browning, prepare the cabbage. Wash the cabbage, peel off any deteriorated outer leaves, then cut into ½-inch slices. Remove the hard core.

❖ Scatter the mustard seed over the bottom of the pot. Add the cabbage and stir it around. Pour in water or white wine to the level of ¼ to ½ inch in the bottom of the pot and cover with a close-fitting lid. Reduce the heat to a simmer. The cabbage will need to cook approximately 30 minutes.

Check the liquid level periodically during the cooking; if necessary, add a bit more water to prevent it from drying out. When the cabbage tests tender, spoon it out, serve the sausages on top, and sit down to a nourishing meal!

The mustard seed softens as it cooks and takes on a nutty flavor, but if it is troublesome, substitute prepared mustard and serve it as a condiment at the table.

Marinated Flank Steak

We are crazy for this steak at my house and end up fighting over the last morsels. You need to plan a few days ahead to prepare this meal; no extra work, just some time to let the tasty marinade do its work. There is enough for several meals for two, hot or cold.

serves 4 to 6
After the steak has been marinated:
start to finish: 10 to 15 minutes

1½ to 2 pounds beef flank steak
3 tablespoons soy sauce
2 tablespoons olive oil
2 or 3 green onions, sliced
2 or 3 cloves garlic, thinly sliced
1 inch fresh ginger, thinly sliced

❖ Lay the meat on a chopping board or butcher block and, using a dinner fork, poke through the meat all over on both sides. This helps tenderize it and allows the marinade really to penetrate.

❖ Then in a shallow dish large enough to hold the meat, mix all the other ingredients together: soy sauce, olive oil, green onion, garlic, and ginger.

❖ Add the meat to the marinade and turn it over several times so it is well coated. Cover the dish and refrigerate for at least one day; two or three days is even better. Turn the meat over on the second day if you think of it.

❖ When ready to cook, turn on the broiler. Take the meat out of the marinade, scrape off the garlic, ginger, and green onions, and place on the broiler pan.

❖ Broil the meat for 4 to 5 minutes on one side, then turn it over and cook another 3 minutes or so for a medium-rare steak. Cook another 2 to 3 minutes for a medium to well-done steak. Let it rest a few minutes on a platter, then slice thinly and serve.

This meat is very good with rice or potatoes, or any fresh vegetable, or a salad and bread. The leftovers are especially good sliced very thinly for a sandwich or cold salad.

Polenta

Corn has sustaining power and even a small serving can see you through to your next meal. Polenta is a smooth, thick cornmeal porridge, like Cream of Wheat and made the same way. It is in that category of great staple foods like rice and potatoes that can go with anything. It is usually served with butter and Parmesan cheese, tomato sauce, or mushroom sauce. In season, try adding tiny cloves of spring garlic to the simmering polenta for a sweet crunchy surprise.

serves 2 to 3
start to finish: 25 to 30 minutes

3 to 4 cups water
½ teaspoon salt
1 cup coarsely ground yellow cornmeal (not cornmeal *flour*)
1 to 2 tablespoons butter
OPTIONAL: Parmesan cheese

❖ Bring the water and salt to a rolling boil in a heavy-bottomed saucepan. Start with 4 cups water for soft polenta, 3 cups for a stiffer texture.

❖ Slowly add the cornmeal, stirring as you do so.

❖ Cook for 2 to 3 minutes at a bubbling boil, stirring continuously until it has thickened evenly. Then reduce the heat and simmer gently for 10 or 15 minutes more, stirring occasionally. If the polenta is too stiff, add a bit of water; if too soupy, cook until it thickens.

❖ Serve it with butter and, if you like, Parmesan cheese.

Note: Leftover polenta is wonderful fried or baked. Pour any remaining polenta into an oiled or buttered bowl or pan. When cool, it will be quite firm; cover and refrigerate. The polenta will keep well for 3 or 4 days.

To cook: turn the polenta out of the bowl or pan onto a cutting board and cut into slices. Gently fry in olive oil on both sides until crisp and lightly browned. A non-stick pan is ideal for this.

It also works very well to bake the slices on an oiled pan or earthenware dish in the oven or toaster oven. If baking, you can top the slices with cheese, which is very good.

Serve plain, or with cheese, tomato sauce, a little leftover stew, some wilted greens—just about anything!

New Tuna Casserole

When you long for the old sinful tuna casserole, but can't face the mushroom soup and potato chips, try this.

serves 4
start to finish: 1 hour and 15 minutes

2 slices oatmeal or whole wheat bread, preferably fresh
⅓ cup ricotta cheese
1 cup milk
2 ounces tofu
1 teaspoon cornstarch
12 ½-ounce can tuna, water or oil packed
5 ounces frozen peas
Salt and pepper
6 pitted black olives
OPTIONAL: butter or oil

❖ Preheat the oven to 350°.

❖ Cut the slices of bread into cubes and put in a blender or food processor. Process to make approximately ¾ cup fresh bread crumbs. Set aside.

❖ In the blender or food processor, briefly blend the ricotta cheese, milk, tofu, and cornstarch. Set aside.

❖ Open the can of tuna and drain, but do not rinse. Set aside.

❖ To assemble the casserole, in a 7- or 8-inch dish: Sprinkle half the bread crumbs on the bottom of the dish. Spread half the tuna, broken into chunks, on top of the bread crumbs. Take out the frozen peas and scatter half on top of the tuna. Lightly season with salt and pepper.

❖ Then make another layer with the remaining tuna, and another layer of peas. Season again with salt and pepper.

❖ Now pour over the milk-cheese-tofu mixture. Tuck the olives in and around the casserole. Sprinkle the remaining half of the bread crumbs on top. Dot with butter if you wish.

❖ Put the casserole, uncovered, in the oven. It will be ready to eat in 45 to 50 minutes. A small salad and some toasted bread are just right with this "new" casserole.

No Stress Rice

A new-old way. An excessive amount of water is used to cook the rice. It absorbs all it can, then rests in the hot water until drained and served. This method reduces the worry of having everything ready at once if you are cooking two or three things for supper.

serves 2 to 4
start to finish: 20 minutes

4 cups water
1 cup rice
OPTIONAL: 1 teaspoon butter
                1 teaspoon salt

❖ Bring the water, and the butter and salt, to a rolling boil over high heat.

❖ Slowly add the rice, stirring as you do so.

❖ Reduce the heat to a simmer and place a lid on the pan. Any time after 20 minutes the rice will be ready and can be served, or it can rest in the simmering water for an hour or more.

❖ When ready to serve, drain the rice in a colander set in the sink.

Note: Sometimes I just want a simple dish of rice as a clean and light meal. A favorite variation is to add ¼ to ½ cup raisins to the pot along with the rice and then finish it in a bowl with a little butter and milk. It's like rice pudding but not so rich.

❖ *Tea and Desserts*

Afternoon Tea
Amish Rice Pudding
Old-fashioned Molasses Cookies
Mémée's Plain Sunday Cake
Easy Creamy Blender Chocolate Frosting
Apple Crisp
Broiled Grapefruit
Memory Lane Desserts

Afternoon Tea

I take tea seriously and approve of tea time in the afternoon. I believe a quiet reviving half hour at tea is worth at least its equivalent in the psychiatrist's office.

As an accompaniment to tea, try a simple graham cracker, a piece of cinnamon toast, or a Marie or arrowroot biscuit with a dot of jam, as was popular in my childhood home. I think spicy gingersnaps and anything chocolate do not go with tea, but this may be a private prejudice.

To condense a lot of information about tea into one sentence—do take tea, make it real tea, not bags, and buy the best you can. If you cannot shop at a tea and coffee specialty shop, you can usually get Typhoo tea in the little red box at large supermarkets. It's a bright English Breakfast blend, small-leafed and tasty, often fresh because of its quick turnover. Lipton black and green loose teas are not superb, but they are honest teas and far superior to any bag. Stay away from any teas that smell of cinnamon or other synthetically flavored blends.

For a small selection of teas at home you might include one English Breakfast; one Earl Grey; one green tea, a Lung Ching perhaps, or a jasmine; and possibly a light black tea—Yunnan, China Black, or Keemun.

Purchase a pottery, porcelain, or glass teapot with a basket or strainer on the inside; avoid aluminum, stainless steel, and silver. The strainer can be removed after the tea steeps 3 or 4 minutes, thus eliminating over-brewed, bitter tea.

❖ To make tea, proceed in the classic way: Fill the teakettle with cold running water. If using a very fine tea, use bottled spring or distilled water. Place the kettle over high heat.

❖ Warm the teapot with hot water from the tap.

❖ When the water in the kettle has *just* come to a *rolling* boil, dump out the hot water in the pot, put the tea-filled strainer or basket in, and pour. Bring the pot to the kettle, not the other way around, as it's very important to pour bubbling, oxygen-filled water over the tea.

    The classic proportion is: 1 teaspoon of tea for each cup of water. Some add "one teaspoon for the pot." In a short time you will figure out how much how much is best for you.

❖ Let the tea steep for 3 to 4 minutes. Set the timer—it's very easy to be distracted.

❖ Remove the strainer, pour yourself a cup, and clap a tea cozy on the pot to keep it nice and hot. Select a goodie to go with the tea, and enjoy yourself.

    The great controversy about adding milk and sugar to tea, I'm glad to announce, has finally been settled. The tea is added to the cup first, and *then* the milk, *not* cream, and sugar are added. I have it on good secondhand authority that this is how the Queen of England does it— and who are we to argue!

Amish Rice Pudding

Don't even think of trying to improve on this one-hundred-year-old recipe. I've tried and have finally concluded that those ladies knew what they were doing.

Be sure the egg yolks are thoroughly beaten before adding the rest of the ingredients. I do this step right in the pan or bowl in which it's baked.

If you think you have actually improved on this recipe, kindly write to me.

serves 2 to 4
start to finish: 1 hour and 30 minutes

2 eggs, separated
½ cup sugar
2 cups milk
1 cup cooked rice, hot or cold
1 tablespoon melted butter
½ cup raisins
½ teaspoon vanilla
2 tablespoons confectioner's sugar
⅛ teaspoon ground nutmeg or cinnamon

❖ Preheat the oven to 325°. Put the egg yolks into a pudding pan or bowl and the whites into a deep-sided mixing bowl. Beat the egg yolks with a hand beater until thickened.

❖ Add the milk and sugar to the beaten yolks and mix. Next add the cooked rice, melted butter, raisins, and vanilla to the egg yolk mixture. Stir everything together.

❖ Beat the whites with clean beaters until they start to become foamy. Slowly add the confectioner's sugar and continue beating until the whites hold their peaks. Tip the bowl and let the whites gently slide out on top of the pudding. Gently spread them over the top.

❖ Sprinkle with nutmeg or cinnamon and bake for 1 hour and 10 minutes.

Serve warm or cold. This pudding needs no added milk or cream.

Old-fashioned Molasses Cookies

These are my grandmother's cookies, made long ago, and remembered so well. I have added measurements for the cinnamon, ginger, and cloves because her recipe card, written in a spare, spidery hand, had only the single appendage: "spices."

makes approximately 30 cookies
start to finish: 1 hour and 30 minutes

¾ cup butter, margarine, or shortening
1 cup sugar
¼ cup dark molasses
2 cups all-purpose flour
2 teaspoons baking soda
½ teaspoon salt
1 teaspoon cinnamon
½ teaspoon ground ginger
¼ to ½ teaspoon ground cloves

❖ Cream together the sugar and butter to form a smooth paste.

❖ Add the egg, beat it into the sugar mixture, and add the molasses.

❖ In a separate bowl, combine the dry ingredients and mix well.

❖ Add the dry ingredients to the molasses mixture and stir until well blended.

❖ The dough is sticky and hard to handle at room temperature. Chill in the refrigerator for a few hours, or, for a shortcut, place the bowl in the freezer for half an hour or so. Then with a spoon, dig out enough dough to form small balls about one inch in diameter.

❖ Roll the balls in a saucer filled with ordinary sugar and place about two inches apart on a lightly greased baking sheet. Bake for about 8 to 10 minutes at 375°. When done, cool on a cake rack or large plate, then place in a cookie jar.

These cookies do not taste sensational the first day—the full flavor and soft, chewy texture ripen on the second or third day. Then they are excellent, more than excellent with a glass of good cold milk.

Mémée's Plain Sunday Cake

This cake is an old-world recipe from a French "Muttie" of my acquaintance. It's simple to make, nearly a one-bowl cake, has few ingredients, and no fat or salt.

Many different toppings—fruit, caramel, and chocolate sauces or icings—go well with it, not to mention ice cream. Vanilla yogurt with a raspberry purée is our favorite—this week.

Best of all, it is wonderful for breakfast when stale, toasted and dipped in café au lait.

makes 1 loaf cake
start to finish: 50 minutes

1 cup sugar
4 eggs, separated
¾ cup sifted all-purpose flour or cake flour
1 tablespoon cornstarch
¾ teaspoon vanilla

❖ Preheat oven to 375°. Add the sugar to the yolks and beat until the mixture is very smooth and whitish in color.

❖ Sift the flour and cornstarch together, add to the sugar-yolk mixture, and blend in gently.

❖ Beat the whites until they are stiff and hold a peak when the beater is removed. Add to the mixture along with the vanilla, and gently fold all together. Do not beat or mix.

❖ Pour into a greased bread loaf pan, approximately 9×5×3 inches, and bake for about 30 minutes. The top will turn a very light brown and have a bubbly texture.

❖ It is done when it springs back when lightly touched.

Let it cool right in the pan and serve in slices directly onto plates.

Easy Creamy Blender Chocolate Frosting

This is the easiest and best chocolate frosting around. It's pretty spectacular to whip this up and spread on graham crackers for visitors or grandkids, and it keeps for weeks in the refrigerator. It makes a good, classic topping to the simple cake on page 86.

The note in The Junior League's Baton Rouge Louisiana Cookbook, *recipe by Mrs. Norman Saurage III, says, "This frosting is absolutely scrumptious." She's right.*

makes 3 cups
start to finish: 5 minutes

6 ounces (6 squares) unsweetened baking chocolate
1½ cups sugar
1 cup evaporated milk
1 teaspoon vanilla
6 tablespoons margarine or butter

❖ Follow these directions *exactly*: Cut chocolate into small pieces. Put all the ingredients in a blender. Cover. Blend at *low* speed until the larger pieces are chopped. Stop the motor and stir. Blend again at *high* speed until frosting becomes thick and creamy.

Apple Crisp

Nothing is quite so good or so popular as fresh, warm apple crisp. This mini easy-to-make favorite can be made in your toaster oven. Try it with vanilla ice cream, fresh cream or half-and-half, or vanilla-flavored yogurt.

serves 1
start to finish: 45 minutes

2 apples
1 tablespoon flour
1 heaping tablespoon brown sugar
1 teaspoon cinnamon
Dash salt
2 to 4 teaspoons water
1 tablespoon butter

❖ Peel, then slice the apples directly into a toaster oven baking tray or dish.

❖ In a small bowl, make a mixture of the flour, brown sugar, cinnamon, and a tiny bit of salt.

❖ Scatter the mixture over the apples. Sprinkle 2 teaspoons water over all, and dab the butter over the top.

❖ Place the tray in the toaster oven and set at 375°.

❖ The crisp will be done in 30 minutes.

Add the greater amount of water if the apples are not very juicy.

Broiled Grapefruit

Broiled grapefruit is good any-time, not only at breakfast. Try it as a dinner dessert warm from the oven, or let it cool and serve at room temperature.

serves 2
start to finish: 15 minutes

1 pink or yellow grapefruit
1 teaspoon brown sugar
OPTIONAL: Pumpkin pie spice

❖ Turn the oven on to broil.

❖ Cut the grapefruit in half, then cut off a shallow slice at the bottom of each half so the grapefruit can sit flat and steady on the broiler pan.

❖ Add 1 teaspoon or more of brown sugar, and, if you like, a sprinkling of pumpkin pie spice in the center of the fruit.

❖ Broil for 12 minutes or so until it looks brown and bubbly.

For another grapefruit dessert, try this: Spread a bit of honey over a grapefruit half, and place a large pinch of crystallized ginger in the center. Chill a few hours before serving.

Memory Lane Desserts

Pumpkin Custard Cups

Pumpkin pie craving always seems to hit in the fall—and for me it is usually accompanied by the ever-present, all-year-long yearning for gingerbread. Here are two shortcuts to same.

❖ Follow the directions on the can of Libby's pumpkin pie filling, for *one* pie, adding evaporated milk and 2 eggs only. Instead of filling a pie shell, pour the mixture into 6 custard cups and bake at 350° for 40 to 45 minutes. Top with some French vanilla ice cream for a real treat.

Valley of the Moon Gingerbread

❖ M. F. K. Fisher suggests this—it's her favorite shortcut to gingerbread nirvana.

Follow your recipe or directions on any gingerbread mix, but add 1 to 2 tablespoons of freshly grated ginger. I think a little shaving of sweet butter is the best thing in the world to top warm gingerbread.

❖ *Catalogue Sources for Special Needs*

Catalogue Sources for Special Needs

This information may be of special interest to older, disabled, or handicapped people. Listed below are two database companies that will provide you with references to catalogues or companies that supply products or literature addressing your specific problem. Also listed are a few catalogues offering a broad selection of helpful items.

My search for equipment sources ended at last when I discovered this amazing company through the Stanford University Rehabilitation Center. All you need to do is call these companies with a description of the kind of thing you require and soon you'll receive ample information, up to 8 pages of information *free*.

ABLEDATA is the largest single source for information on disability-related consumer products, with over 15,000 commercially available products listed from over 1,800 manufacturers. Products are included from 15 categories of assistive technology, including Personal Care, Communication, Transportation, and Recreation. A custom search of the database helps you to locate and compare similar products for yourself, your family, or your client. Staff is available from 8:30 A.M. to 5:00 P.M., Monday through Friday to assist you with any searches you may need.

You may call, write, or visit the Adaptive Equipment Center at Newington Children's Hospital and they will complete an ABLEDATA search for you. Contact ABLEDATA, Adaptive Equipment Center, Newington Children's Hospital, 181 East Cedar Street, Newington, CT 06111. Phone 800-344-5405 or 203-667-5405 voice or TTD.

Another company for rehabilitation products is KAPR Ltd. They can send you the *Nottingham Rehab Catalog*—a very complete source for aids of all kinds from Nottingham, England. For information, contact: KAPR, 11429 E. 20th Street, Tulsa, OK 74128. Phone 800-633-4458. FAX 918-234-786. They, too, will send a small amount of information free of charge. For a modest fee you can obtain more.

For specific information on arthritis, contact the *National Arthritis Foundation* for the arthritis center nearest you. Write National Arthritis Foundation, National Headquarters, 1314 Spring Street, Atlanta, GA 30309. Phone 404-872-7100.

A partial list of some helpful catalogues:

Comfortably Yours
61 West Hunter Avenue, Maywood, NJ 07607. Phone 201-368-0400.
Mostly women's clothing, some bedroom and bathroom items.

Solutions
P.O. Box 6878, Portland, OR 97228. Phone 1-800-342-9988.
A general catalogue: devices for the car, bedroom, garden, and home. Some clothing.

Mature Wisdom
Hanover, PA 17333-0028. Phone 1-800-621-5800.
A general catalogue: some clothing, self-help devices, travel aids, some furniture, and kitchen aids.

Brookstone Homewares
5 Vose Road, Peterborough, NH 03458. Phone 603-924-9541.
Devices for kitchen and home use.

ROBERT MESSICK

Helen Gustafson's first book was *Dinner's Ready, Mom* (Ten Speed/Celestial Arts). She fell into Berkeley's food world in the 70s after a decade of teaching school. She lives with her family in Berkeley, California.